THERE IS A RAINBOW BEHIND EVERY DARK CLOUD

The Center for Attitudinal Healing

CELESTIAL ARTS
Millbrae, California

1

Celestial Arts
231 Adrian Road
Millbrae, California 94030

First Printing, July 1978
Second Printing, August 1979

Made in the United States of America

Library of Congress Cataloging in Publication Data

Center for Attitudinal Healing, Tiburon, Calif.
    There is a rainbow behind every dark cloud.

    SUMMARY: Eleven children share their experiences with terminal illness, especially the ways they helped each other cope with the prospect of their own death.
    1. Sick children—Psychology—Juvenile literature.   2. Termi-nally ill children—Psychology—Juvenile literature.   3. Death—Psychological aspects—Juvenile literature.   [1. Sick—Psychol-ogy.   2. Death— Psychological aspects.   3. Children's writings]   I. Title.
RJ47.5.C42 1978   155.9'37   79-9453
ISBN 0-89087-253-8

2 3 4 5 6 7 - 86 85 84 83 82 81

THANK YOU

We wish to thank Bruce Davis, Genny Davis, Betsy Golkin, Gloria Murray, Patsy Robinson, Roger Smith, Tom Pinkson and Kate Amatruda who have been a part of our group at the Center for At-titudinal Healing in Tiburon, California.

We did all the pictures ourselves in this book except those that are signed by Mr. Jack Keeler, a professional cartoonist, who met with us a few times and listened to our story.

The spiritual framework and philosophy that our group was based on came from the writing in "A Course in Miracles" published by the Foundation for Inner Peace, 230 Central Park South, #14E, New York, NY 10019.

INTRODUCTION

This is a book written for children like us who have gotten sick with cancer, leukemia, and other sicknesses where you are scared you might die.

We find as we help each other, we help ourselves.

We hope that writing this small book will help you gain through sharing our experiences

Andrea Dezendorf—8 years
Kenneth Estrada—8 years
Greg Harrison—11 years
Steven Johnsen—9 years
Rory Kittleson—9 years
David Martin—12 years
Jennifer Meyers—12 years
Joseph Orr—12 years
Nancy Peugh—19 years
Mike Stevens—13 years
Tinman Walker—18 years

FOREWORD

This book is the result of group meetings of children who had to face life and death situations because of their illness. The group started in October, 1976 at the Center for Attitudinal Healing in Tiburon, California.

We think healing, or "getting well," means being happy and peaceful inside. We think healing takes place when we feel nothing but love inside and when we are no longer scared or feeling bad about anything.

Letting go of the past means letting the past completely disappear and not hanging on to it. It means living each second as if it were the only time there was. It is living in the "now." It is making this day count.

The adult volunteers and children have been equally interested in healing themselves by finding ways of getting rid of their fears. We have seen each other equally as student/teacher, teacher/student.

We have found that love is the fuel that allows for the joining of minds, and that age is not a factor in telling us who our teachers are.

We are most grateful to the children and co-workers in our group, the children's families, their physicians, and the many others who have been so cooperative and helpful to us.

GERALD G. JAMPOLSKY, M.D.
PAT TAYLOR

3

TABLE OF CONTENTS

PART I

WHAT WE EXPERIENCED

CHAPTER I

Before We Got Sick

Before we got sick we could run fast, play hard, and we were happy.

Before we got sick we didn't think anything could stop us from having fun with our families, friends and everything around us.

Before we got sick we didn't use words like "hope" and didn't talk about God very much.

We thought our parents could make anything bad go away.

Before we got sick we didn't feel helpless but after we got sick, we did.

DRAW A PICTURE SHOWING YOURSELF BEFORE YOU GOT SICK

Before I got sick
I was very shy.

I used to
be afraid of
monsters.

8

Andrea Dezendorf

Foot Ball is fun to.

David Martin

9

I Like rideing
In my Dads truck

10

David Martin

(Before we got sick)

Jack Keeler

11

CHAPTER II

The Day We Got Sick

A lot of kids in our group have leukemia, and they frequently got stomach aches, headaches, felt weak and bruised easily.

Some of the kids had cancer and in the beginning were in a lot of pain.

One boy in our group had a bad accident which was sudden and very painful.

When we all found what was really wrong with us, we were very scared.

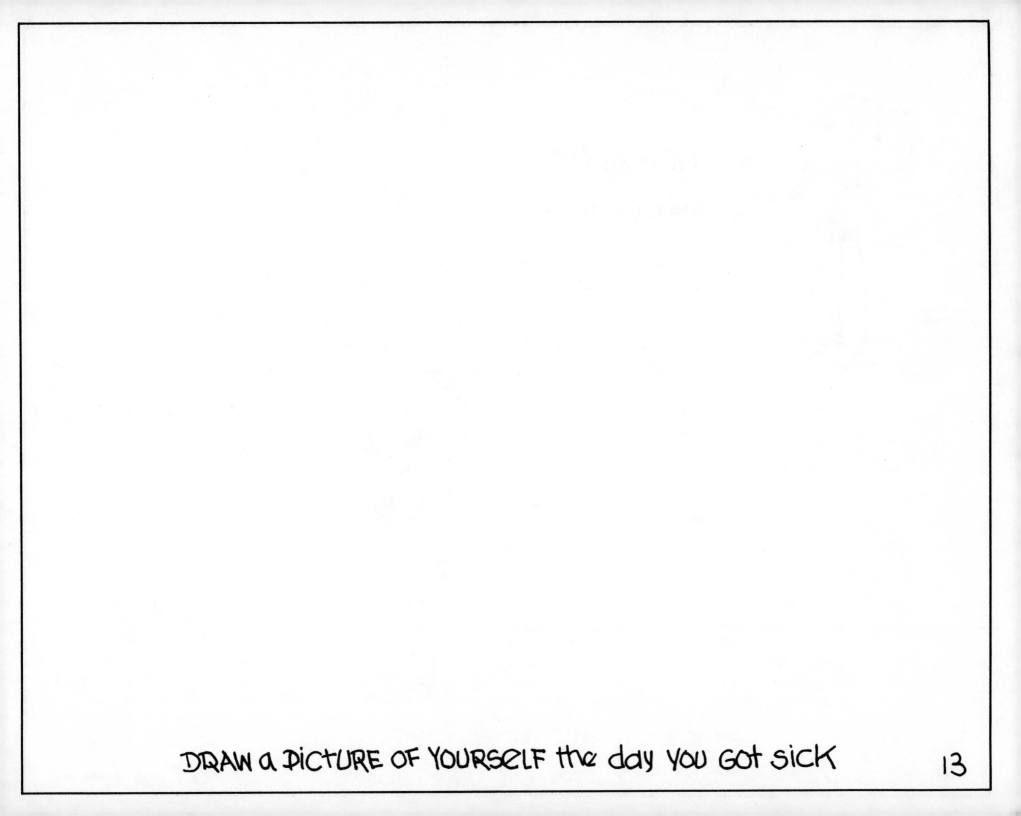

DRAW a PICTURE OF YOURSELF the day YOU GOT SICK

The Pain is in my side.

Mom I don't feel good.

14

David Martin

CHAPTER III

Seeing the Doctor for the First Time

The worst part of seeing the doctor was all the jabs of the needle. Some of us started crying when we got our shots. The doctor had always made us feel better in the past, but this time he sent us to the hospital. They couldn't tell most of us, for sure, what we had or if we would get better. Some of us were really scared that we were going to die.

16   DRAW A Picture of yourself seeing the doctor for the first time

Andrea Dezendorf

18

CHAPTER IV

Going to the Hospital

What bothered us most about being in the hospital was feeling alone. We didn't like being separated from our parents, brothers and sisters and friends. We also didn't like the shots and the tests. Many of us found going into the X-ray room and the operating room scary. It also wasn't fun to watch them stick needles in you and connect transfusions to them. Following an accident, one of us had the following experience: "I was riding my bike and a truck and my bike hit each other. I had 54 stitches on my face. My head had to be shaved. My doctor thought I might have a clot on my brain. I was knocked out cold for 81 days. Everyone thought I might die, but I didn't!"

In the hospital time dragged. We were bothered by the lonely nights. There wasn't anyone to talk with. There seemed to be nothing to do. All of us missed home a lot.

Most of us found that praying helped us not be scared.

DRAW a picture of yourself in the hospital

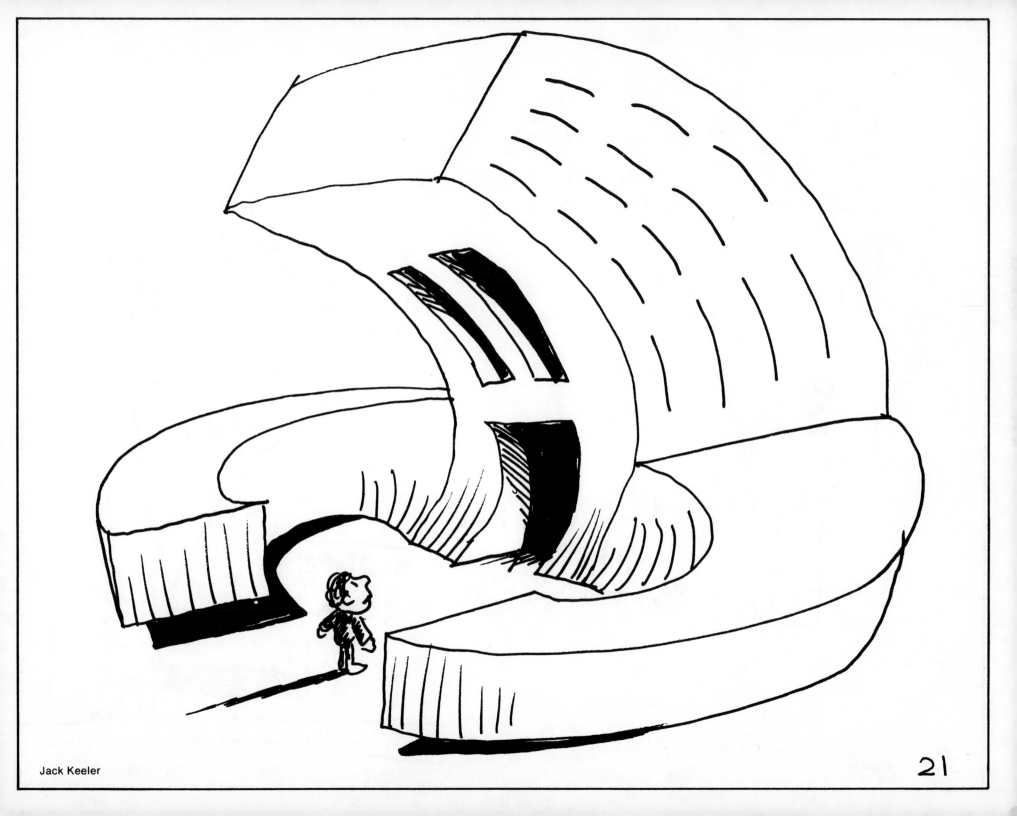

Jack Keeler

21

David Martin

Andrea Dezendorf

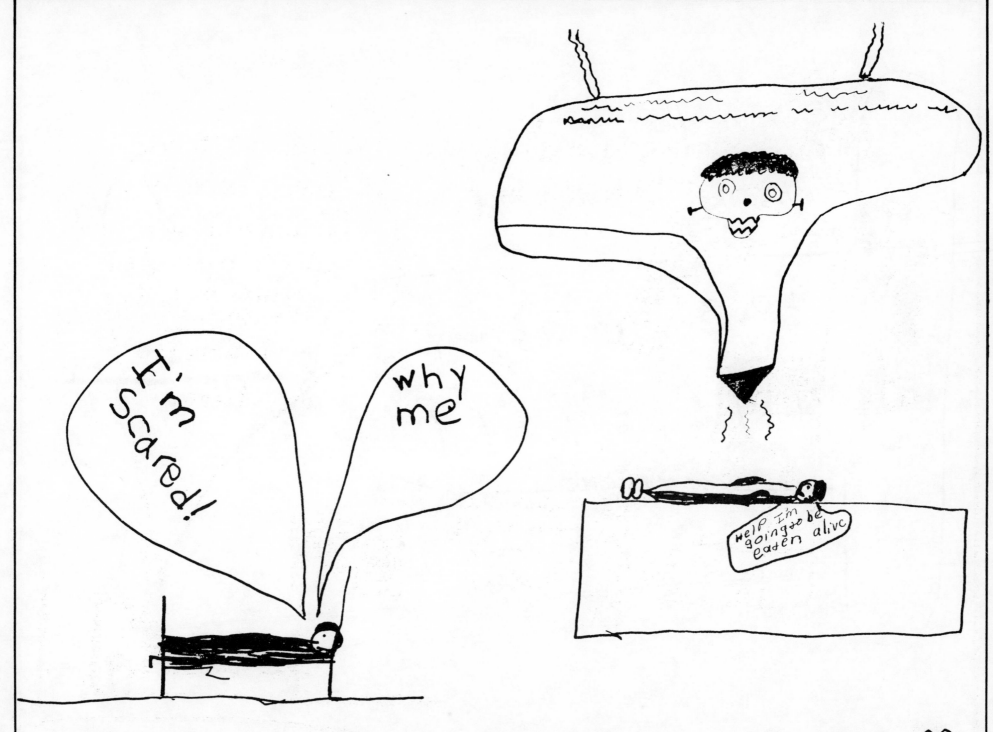

Some needles felt like fishhooks

40 35 30 25 20 15 10 5

cm Dispose of Properly.

24

Mike Stevens

Jack Keeler

Greg Harrison

28

Jack Keeler

29

30

Jack Keeler

CHAPTER V

Hearing the News

After we were told what our sickness was and that we might die from it, we were mad that it happened to us. The "not knowing" if we were going to get well really bothered us. Hearing that we were going to get lots of shots and lose our hair also scared us.

We did not look forward to getting X-ray therapy and chemotherapy because lots of times it made us feel worse, even though we knew it was given to us to make us well.

It was hard for most of us to talk about how we felt inside. And it was hard for us to find someone who would really listen without being afraid. Sometimes the questions we were afraid to ask were: "Am I going to die?" "What is dying like?"

We knew certain questions would bring tears to our parents' eyes so we learned not to ask those questions. All of us seemed to want to protect our parents.

At the same time, we wanted to be physically close to our parents most of the time. Lots of times we didn't want them out of our sight.

The nurses were great at the hospital. They made us feel comfortable, but we all wanted to go home.

Draw a picture of Yourself hearing the news about your illness

WHY me!

Why not someone else. Why Do I always get sick.

33

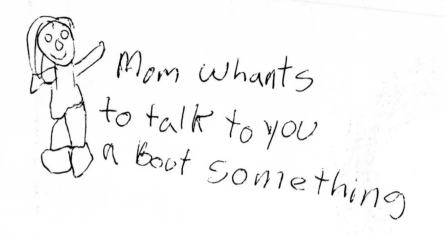

Mom whants to talk to you a boot something

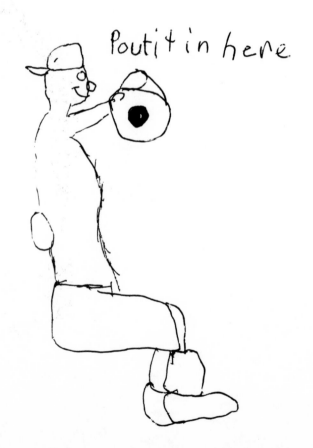

Poutit in here

34

Jack Keeler

35

CHAPTER VI

Homecoming

It was really very nice coming home to your family, your friends and your pets. It was good seeing your room and your house, knowing it was still there.

Everything felt safe and warm, and everyone and everything seemed to love us. Our brothers and sisters never looked so good. Our mother fixed our favorite meal. It felt good to feel like a person again and not a pin cushion. We felt like a king or queen. Some of our brothers and sisters thought we were being spoiled. They thought being sick meant you got your own way.

Those of us with leukemia, at times were put in isolation, which meant we couldn't go to school or be with other kids. Our white blood count was low and the doctor was afraid we would get an infection and not be able to battle it.

Being in isolation meant that you were lonely. It became easy to feel sorry for ourselves, but it didn't usually last long.

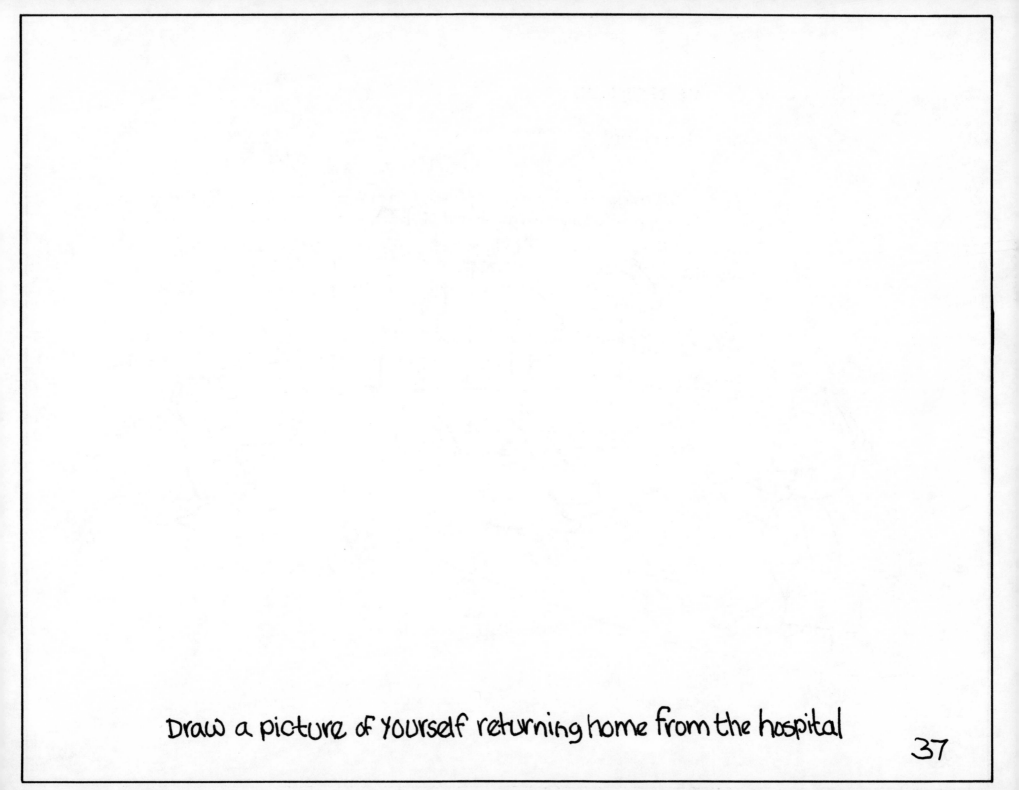

Draw a picture of yourself returning home from the hospital

37

38

Put in isolation couldn't play with other kids

39

CHAPTER VII

Back to the Doctor's Office

Some of us who had cancer, or leukemia, had to have chemotherapy and X-ray treatments, blood tests and bone marrow tests.

We knew they were important things to be done, but they were not much fun. We spent a lot of time waiting and hoping that the tests would come out okay. Our doctors told us the truth about everything and we learned to trust them.

Lots of times our parents seemed to hide behind smiling faces but were really more worried and afraid than we were.

Being stuck by needles, "not knowing," and waiting for the results were the worst things of all.

For most of us it was scary going back to the doctor's office. There was always the thought that we might have it again and have to go through all the shots and tests and X-rays again.

Draw a picture of Yourself going back to the doctor's office

Sometimes you fell liK a Pincusion after so many shots

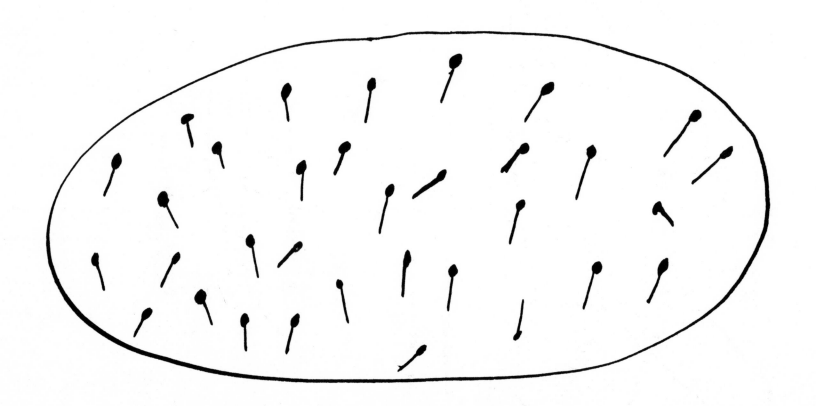

42

43

44

Jack Keeler

CHAPTER VIII

Going Back to School

Most of us had two feelings at the same time: wanting to go back to school and being scared of going back.

It was really tough going back to school when you didn't have any hair. All the kids asked us, "What happened?" "Where is all your hair?" "Why are you wearing that hat or that wig?"

Sometimes we met some guy who acted like a jerk and tried to pull our hat off. Sometimes we ended up fighting.

We didn't like feeling different. We also felt dumb because we missed so much school and we thought we would never catch up.

We were also mad because we missed out on sports.

The kids kept asking us what was wrong with us and lots of times we didn't know what to say. So lots of times we didn't say anything. We didn't feel like talking about it.

Draw a Picture of yourself going back to school

46

48

Jack Keeler

Jack Keeler

49

PART II

CHOICES YOU HAVE
IN HELPING YOURSELF

We found we could decide to be happy "inside" even though we didn't like what was happening to us on the outside.

CHAPTER IX

Things You Can Do About Your Feelings

First of all, you can choose to help yourself by speaking up and saying anything that is on your mind. Hiding your feelings just makes you more scared.

So don't hide the way you feel. Just be yourself. Don't fight your angry feelings. Just accept them and then they can quickly go away.

It's okay to cry. It's okay not to like hospitals and shots, to be homesick, to be upset about being lonely, and to be mad that this is happening to you.

It's okay to feel sorry for yourself and to be mad at the world and everyone in it. And it's okay to talk about death and your fears about it.

We found it helpful to find other kids who have similar problems and to meet with them. We have found that, as we helped each other, we have helped ourselves. We have fun and don't think about being afraid.

It is helpful to find you are not alone, and that there are other kids just like you who are going through the same thing. Other kids have the same feelings you do about losing their hair. Kids can be more helpful than adults because they talk your language. Kids can also understand without your having to use words.

When other kids tease you, you can pay no attention to them; you can fight them; or you can choose to see that they are scared. (We found that sometimes a kid teases you because they are the ones who are scared.)

Draw a picture of yourself showing your feelings

Choices You have in Helping Yourself.

Jack Keeler

53

54

Kenneth Estrada

55

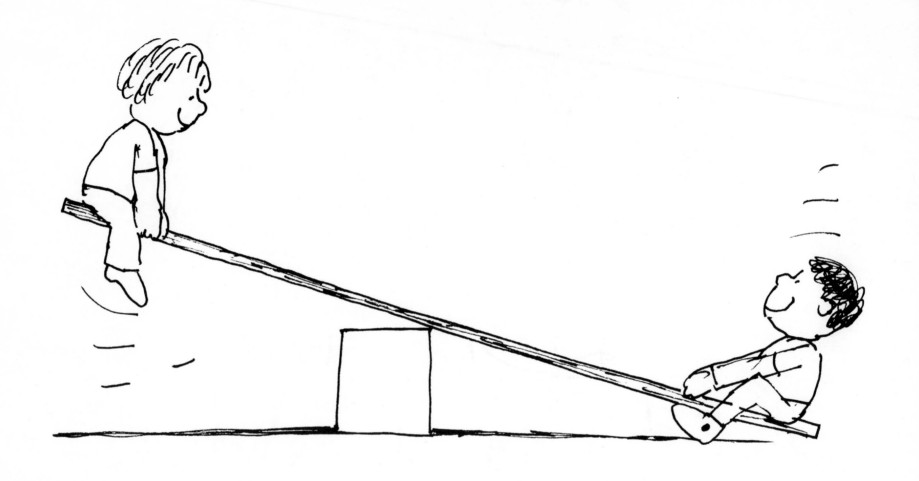

we help each other and have fun.

Jack Keeler

Don't hide the way you feel.. Just be yourself.

CHAPTER X

"Letting Go" and Forgiving

When we learned not to look at yesterday and tomorrow, we found that we weren't so scared.

Forgiveness, to us, meant not blaming anyone for anything. It was tempting to blame the doctor when he had trouble finding our vein. It was also tempting to blame our parents, brothers and sisters, teachers and friends for lots of things. "Letting go" of the past (not hanging on to it) and forgiving everyone and everything sure helped a lot in not being so afraid. We learned to say, "Now is the only time there is."

Draw a Picture of Yourself "Letting go" and Forgiving

this instant is the only time that counts.

Jack Keeler

Forgivness is forgiving the doctor if he puts a needle in and finds out he put it in the wrong place and has to put it in a second time. Just letting the inceadent float away.

Mike Stevens

This is Try Lopose   she is very happy
with me any friends. She forgived Laponusey
for biting here hard. forgiveness is not
holeding a gruge to eney one. It's
not anger or harsh mean talk to eney
one but nicesness and mild temperdness

CHAPTER XI

Using Your Imagination to Help Yourself

Another choice you have is to decide not to be afraid by using your imagination in a way that works for you.

We all found that using your active imagination really helps.

For example, either when you are in the hospital or very sick at home and are very lonely, just sort of daydream about something pleasant. Just let your imagination run away with yourself. Picture in your mind something you really want to do when you get well, like go to Disneyland, and make it seem real.

Or when you are ready to get a shot you can imagine that your arm is numb from rolling in the snow. And when you do this, guess what? The needle won't hurt you so much.

Some of us played with imaginary playmates. We went on make believe picnics and beach parties. We learned that, by using our imagination, we could do anything.

The following are some imagination exercises we found helpful:

Close your eyes and picture in your mind a large garbage can. Put into the garbage can any fear and anything bad that has happened in the past. See a large yellow balloon, filled with gas, being attached to your garbage can. See your garbage can go up into the sky and disappear. We found this was a quick way of getting rid of things in the past that bugged us.

Another imagination exercise is to close your eyes and imagine that you are taking your brain out of your head. Get a hose and imagine that you are washing away all the fears and bad memories of the past. Then put your brain back in your head and picture yourself feeling okay.

Some of us were in the hospital for a long, long time because of an accident. We found that, by using our imagination, we could keep a picture in our mind of a rainbow on the other side of a stormy cloud. This helped give us hope and patience.

Some of us with leukemia also learned to use our imagination to make pictures in our mind of good cells beating up the bad cells.

Draw a picture of yourself using your imagination to help yourself

64

Jack Keeler

65

me riding my elphant

66

67

The bad cells eating ~~up~~ up the good
cells and the good cells eating up the
bad cells but the good cells won.

Joseph Orr

fish are Like ~~cells~~

cells. The Big Good ~~Cells~~ ~~cells~~
eat up the Bad cells.

Greg Harrison

72

David Martin

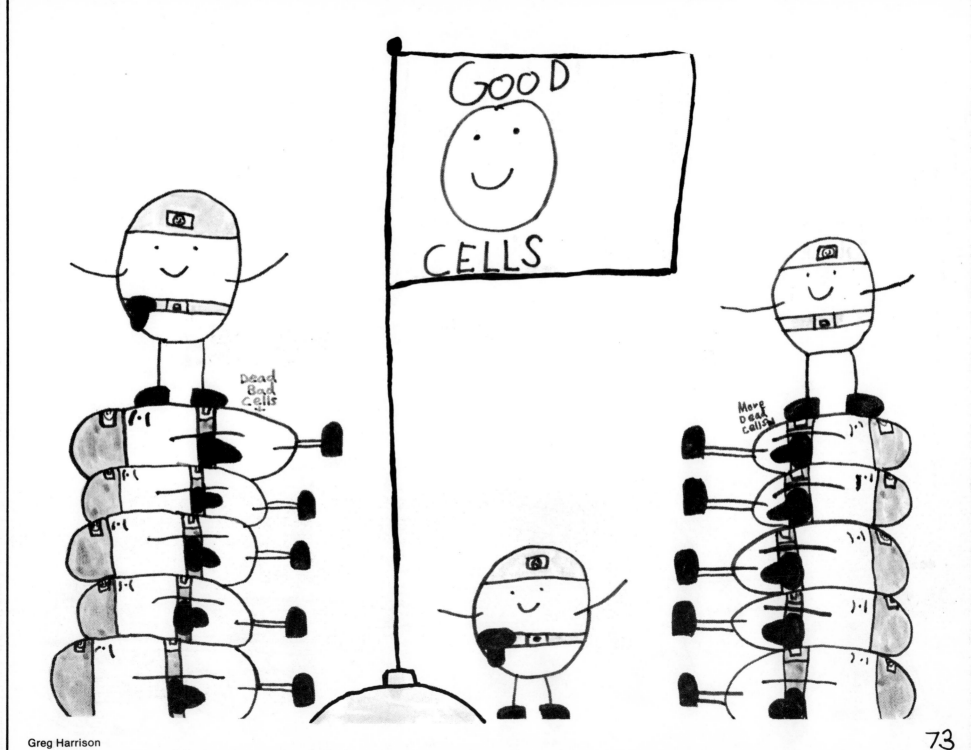

Greg Harrison

Greg Harrison

75

76

Greg Harrison

THE FIGHT FOR LIFE!

Greg Harrison

CHAPTER XII

Using Your Dreams to Help You

We found that we could choose to have our dreams help us. For example, one of us had the same dream happen night after night. It was scary. It was a boy climbing a ladder into the sky ending nowhere. Then there was a space machine in the sky over him. There were gremlins on it throwing rocks at the boy, trying to knock him down.

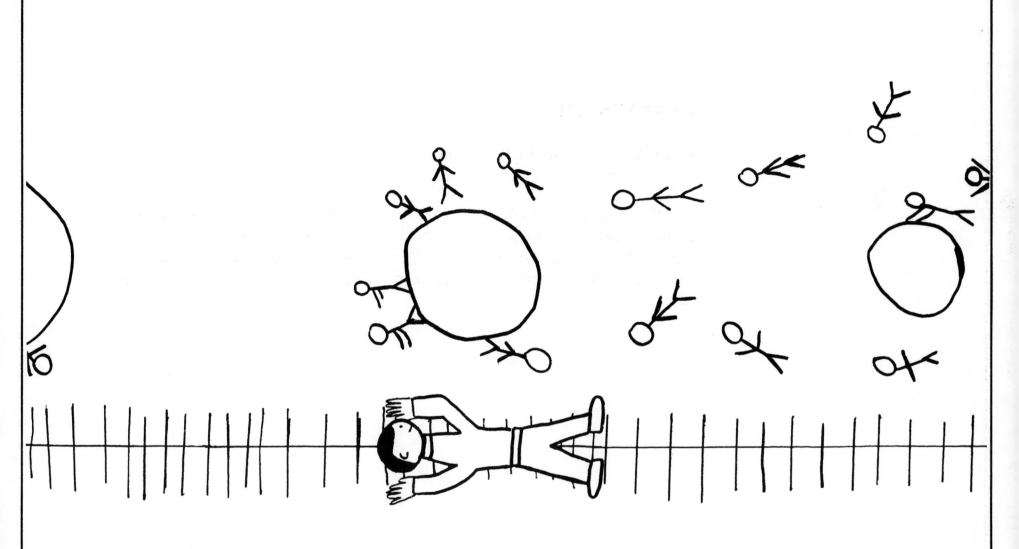

DReam: Picture of boy on ladder going nowhere

This picture shows the ladder ending in heaven. The boy is happy. He is making the space machine move fast so the gremlins would fall off. Some fell off in parachutes so they wouldn't get hurt.

He went home and dreamed the dream that he drew. His scary dreams then stopped.

IT IS IMPORTANT TO KNOW THAT YOUR MIND CAN CHOOSE TO HAVE A DREAM END ANY WAY YOU WANT.

Dream: Boy on ladder going to Heaven — and gremlins
Falling back to earth.

CHAPTER XIII

Talking About Death Can Help

We all found it helpful to talk about death. It seemed easier to talk about being afraid of dying with other kids than to talk about it with adults. Lots of times adults get nervous, change the subject, and tell us that we shouldn't think of things like that.

Drawing pictures about what we thought death was like and talking about the pictures with each other made it less scary to talk about.

It was helpful to find out how other kids looked at death.

One of us thought, "When you die, your body leaves you and your soul goes to heaven. There it joins other souls and becomes one soul. And sometimes the soul comes back to earth and acts as a guardian angel to someone." We all seemed to like that way of looking at death.

Draw your own picture of what you think death is like

"People being hanged"

"a grave yard & heaven"

"Death is like
jumping off a diving
board & disappearing."

86

"Death is like being in the light everywhere"

87

Greg Harrison

CHAPTER XIV

Praying Can Help

Most of us found that praying was of great help. It made us not feel alone. It helped us to find faith and hope that we were safe. When we put everything in God's hands it helped us know that everything would be okay. It really made the fear go away. It made us happy and peaceful inside.

Draw a picture of yourself praying

90

I am praying because
I am sick and I want
to feel better

91

92

CHAPTER XV

Summary

In summary, we think that your mind can do anything. You can learn to control your mind and decide to be happy "inside" with a smiling heart, in spite of what happens to you on the "outside."

Whether you are sick or well, when you give help and love to others, it makes you feel warm and peaceful inside. We learned that, when you give love, you receive it at the same time.

And letting go of the past and forgiving everyone and everything sure helps you not be afraid.

Remember that you are love. So let your love expand and love yourself and everyone. When you love and really feel joined with everyone, everything and with God, you can feel happy and safe inside.

And don't forget, when you have total Faith, that we are always connected to each other in love, you will surely find a rainbow on the other side of any dark cloud.

Draw a picture of yourself happy and loving yourself and others.

Rory Kittleson

95

I feel good under a rainbow. when I'm Happy.

96

Rory Kittleson